A Girlfriend Is...

Original Text and Artwork by

For Giving Souls™

HARVEST HOUSE PUBLISHERS

EUGENE, OREGON

A Girlfriend Is...

Copyright © 2006 by Harvest House Publishers
Eugene, Oregon 97402

ISBN-13: 978-0-7369-1519-9
ISBN-10: 0-7369-1519-2

For Giving Souls™ © 2006 by G Studios, LLC. For Giving Souls Trademarks
owned by G Studios, LLC, Newport Beach, CA USA and used by Harvest
House Publishers, Inc., under authorization. For more information regarding
art prints featured in this book, please contact:

G Studios, LLC
4500 Campus Drive, Suite 200
Newport Beach, CA 92660
949.261.1300
www.gstudiosllc.com

Design and production by Garborg Design Works, Minneapolis, Minnesota

Printed in China

06 07 08 09 10 11 12 / LP / 10 9 8 7 6 5 4 3 2 1

TO

_____

Your friend always,

_____

Forever...

Friends are those special people we do life
with. And because of you,
life has a new meaning. Thank you for
touching my life in a way
that only you could. Your friendship is a
beautiful gift to be treasured.

A girlfriend

Never believe that a few caring people can't change the world. For, indeed, that's all who ever have.

MARGARET MEAD

Too often we underestimate the power of a touch, a smile, a kind word, a listening ear, an honest compliment, or the smallest act of caring, all of which have the potential to turn a life around.

LEO BUSCAGLIA

Because of you...my life has been touched in a meaningful way. Because of your faith in me I have overcome the challenges that used to stop me from pursuing what matters. You are a hero to me.

is...caring.

A girlfriend

Thank you for being an incredible
friend, for loving and not judging,
for listening and not talking, for
being honest and not telling me
what I want to hear. You're a great
person and an amazing friend.

*Friendship, of itself a holy tie,
Is made more sacred by adversity.*

JOHN DRYDEN

By friendship you mean the
greatest love, the greatest
usefulness, the most open
communication, the noblest
sufferings, the severest truth,
the heartiest counsel, and
the greatest union of minds
of which brave men and
women are capable.

JEREMY TAYLOR

is...honest.

A girlfriend

Friends are those special people we get to experience life with...Because of you my life has been touched in a profound way. You have been a pillar of strength, a shoulder to cry on, and a hand to hold. You are a precious gift to me.

Some friendships are made by nature, some by contract, and some by souls.

JEREMY TAYLOR

is...a soulsister.

The glory of friendship is not the outstretched hand, nor the kindly smile, nor the joy of companionship; it is the spiritual inspiration that comes to one when he discovers that someone else believes in him and is willing to trust him with his friendship. My friends have come unsought. The great God gave them to me.

RALPH WALDO EMERSON

Friendship! Mysterious cement of the soul! Sweet'ner of life, and solder of society!

ROBERT BLAIR

A girlfriend
is...thoughtful.

Caring about others, running the risk of feeling, and leaving an impact on people, brings happiness.

HAROLD KUSHNER

The responsibilities of friendship? To talk...and to listen.

ROSIE THOMAS

Talking with a friend is nothing else but thinking aloud.

JOSEPH ADDISON

When a friend is in trouble, don't annoy him by asking if there is anything you can do. Think up something appropriate and do it.

EDWARD W. HOWE

A girlfriend

I think the next best thing to solving a problem is finding some humor in it.

FRANK A. CLARK

From quiet homes and first beginning,
Out to the undiscovered ends,
There's nothing worth the wear of winning,
But laughter and the love of friends.

HILAIRE BELLOC

A sense of humor is a major defense against minor troubles.

MIGNON MCLAUGHLIN

is...funny.

A belly laugh is
good for the soul...

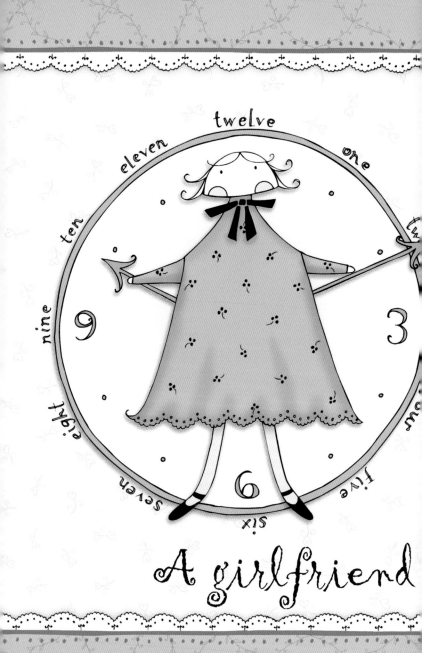

A girlfriend

I value the friend who for me finds time
on his calendar, but I cherish the friend
who for me does not consult his calendar.

ROBERT BRAULT

It's the
friends you
can call up
at 4 a.m.
that matter.

MARLENE DIETRICH

There is nothing on this earth more
to be prized than true friendship.

SAINT THOMAS AQUINAS

is...spontaneous.

A girlfriend
is...forgiving.

Forgive

Friends are worth forgiving.

"A friend is the one who comes in when the whole world has gone out." Even as David thanked God for Jonathan and praised him in well-remembered lines, so have we abundant reasons to thank God today for friends and to resolve to keep these friendships in constant repair.

EDGAR DeWITT JONES

Forgiveness is the key to action and freedom.

HANNAH ARENDT

Grace is essential—it allows people to fail and truly be forgiven.

You're one of the most amazing people I know. You're hip, stylish, fashionable, talented, intelligent, and fun to be with. The gift you are to me is...fun, trustworthy, loyal, and trendy. I love you, girly girl.

It is not so much our friends' help that helps us, as the confidence of their help.

EPICURUS

Be willing to share your secrets; they may be what sets another free.

Great souls by instinct to each other turn,
Demand alliance, and in friendship burn.

JOSEPH ADDISON

A girlfriend is...trustworthy.

A girlfriend

Leave impressions that will bring
life and cause hope in another's soul.

Friends
help the
rainy
days seem
brighter...

But friendship is precious, not only in
the shade, but in the sunshine of life,
and thanks to a benevolent arrangement
the greater part of life is sunshine.

THOMAS JEFFERSON

is...encouraging.

A girlfriend

Friend, I admire you for how you live your life, how you love your family, and yet still have time for friends. I love the fact that you make time for every person that truly matters in your life. Thank you for being such a thoughtful, faithful friend.

Charity is a virtue of the heart, and not of the hands.

JOSEPH ADDISON

Greater love hath no man than this, that a man lay down his life for his friends.

THE BOOK OF JOHN

is...giving

Give the world the best
you have and the best
will come back to you.

AUTHOR UNKNOWN

*God has
given us two
hands—one to
receive with and the
other to give with. We
are not cisterns made
for hoarding; we are
channels of sharing.*

BILLY GRAHAM

23

24

A girlfriend is...silly.

The best friend a girl can have is one who knows how to have a girly good time.

It is one of the blessings of old friends that you can afford to be stupid with them.

RALPH WALDO EMERSON

Risk looking silly... in order to put a smile in someone's heart.

When I think about you, I get a big smile that takes over my face! I cherish you and I love our time together. Being with you is fun, real, tender, entertaining, meaningful, and always memorable. Thanks for being easy to be with and a safe place in the storms of life.

She is a friend of mind. She gather me, man. The pieces I am, she gather them and give them back to me in all the right order. It's good, you know, when you got a woman who is a friend of your mind.

TONI MORRISON

Love must be sincere. Hate what is evil; cling to what is good. Be devoted to one another in brotherly love. Honor one another above yourselves.

THE BOOK OF ROMANS (NIV)

A girlfriend
is...sincere.

A girlfriend

Words spoken
in love can
change the world.

A true
friend
reaches for
your hand
and touches
your heart.

AUTHOR UNKNOWN

It is possible to give without loving,
but it is impossible to love without giving.

RICHARD BRAUNSTEIN

Life is to be fortified
by many friendships.
To love and to be
loved is the greatest
happiness of existence.

SYDNEY SMITH

is...loving.

A girlfriend

Friends are worth fighting for, worth pursuing, worth investing in, and worth keeping.

Forever...

Long friendships are like jewels—polished over time to become beautiful and enduring.

CELIA BRAYFIELD

Friends are gifts from God. It can happen in a day and last a lifetime.

We've been friends forever. I suppose that can't be true. There must have been a time before we became friends but I can't remember it. You are in my first memory and all my best memories ever since.

LINDA MACFARLANE

s...forever.

A true friend
is forever a friend.

GEORGE MACDONALD